Presented to

_____

from

_____

_____ *19*____

The King's Workers

A Bible Book about Serving

Library of Congress Cataloging-in-Publication Data

Hollingsworth, Mary, 1947-
The king's workers : a Bible book about serving / concept by
Cheryl Rico and Ginger Knight ; illustrated by Mary Grace
Eubank ; text by Mary Hollingsworth.
p. cm.
Summary: Children describe, in verse, what they want to be
and how their future occupations would serve God.
ISBN 0-8499-0827-2 : $7.99
1. Vocation—Juvenile literature. [1. Occupations. 2. Christian
life.] I. Rico, Cheryl, 1951- . II. Knight, Ginger, 1954-
III. Eubank, Mary Grace, ill. IV. Title.
BV4740.H567   1990
242'.62—dc20   90-32208
                                                            CIP
                                                            AC
Printed in the United States of America.
0123 9LB 987654321

The King's Workers

A Bible Book about Serving

Concept by: Cheryl Rico and Ginger Knight
Illustrated by: Mary Grace Eubank
Text by: Mary Hollingsworth

WORD PUBLISHING
Dallas · London · Vancouver · Melbourne

Dear Parent,

Kids really do spend a lot of time wondering what they will "be" when they grow up. It is a question that warrants much concern and positive shaping on your part.

The King's Workers brings a unique outlook to the field of occupations. It teaches children that every job is good so long as it is done with a servant's heart. You will find no other book that so beautifully teaches this important principle.

As you know, dreams do not always come true; not every child will be a doctor, lawyer or astronaut. That's why it is imperative to children's self-esteem that they master the concept that service is more important and pleasing to God than the actual profession. This teaching will also aid children in not becoming unduly proud and in understanding others in less prestigious professions.

The King's Workers will be a favorite book for all children with its captivating art by Sesame Street artist, Mary Grace Eubank.

Author Mary Hollingsworth keeps the text simple, to the point, and fun to read with her delightful rhymes.

We hope *The King's Workers* will become an invaluable tool to help your children understand occupations, and to help them realize that serving God and others makes any job worthwhile.

The Publisher

The King sent out a royal call
to kingdom kids: "Come one; come all!"
He smiled and said, "Please answer Me:
When you grow up, what will you be?"

So, one by one they all filed by.
Some kids were brave, but some were shy,
They all described what work they'd do
To serve the King and others, too.

DOCTOR/NURSE
"When I grow up, I want to be
A doctor who helps others see
Or nurse who makes folks good as new
When they have chicken pox or flu."

TEACHER
"O King, a teacher's who I'll be
To help kids learn their ABC's
They'll read the Bible, start to end,
And share its message with a friend."

ASTRONAUT
"Perhaps I'll be an astronaut;
Exploring space will be my lot.
As stars fly by and comets nod
I'll try to see the face of God."

CLOTHING DESIGNER
"Your people must have clothes to wear;
So, I'll design them with a flair —
In faded jeans or flowered skirt,
I'll dress them up for play and work.

FARMER
"I'll work the land," said one small lad,
"Just like my grandpa and my dad.
My wheat crops will keep people fed
So they won't starve from lack of bread."

WIFE/MOTHER

"A wife and mom's the job for me—
I want to serve my family.
I'll make our home a happy place
By putting smiles on every face."

ARTIST
"Fine art's the work that I will choose.
I'll paint with reds and greens and blues
To catch the glory of God's sky
Or show his pretty butterfly."

FIRE FIGHTER
"Quick action! That's the way I'll live,
For fighting fire's my gift to give.
I'll rescue people from the flames!
Yes, Fireman Freddy is my name."

COACH
"It's teamwork that the world needs most,
Not braggers who just want to boast;
So I will teach kids as they play
To work together day by day."

LAWYER

"A lawyer should be good and kind;
So, that's how I will use my mind.
I'll serve my God and fellow man
By using laws the best I can."

POLICE PERSON
"O King, I want to keep your peace;
So, I will join our town's police.
I'll keep folks safe in every place,
Enforcing law but showing grace."

MECHANIC
"I want to fix a truck or car—
When it breaks down or won't run far.
'Mechanic' is the sign I'll show
And keep God's people on the go."

REALTOR
"Well, I'd like real estate a lot—
Just helping families find a spot
The perfect home and perfect land
Where love and joy live hand in hand."

RESTAURANT WORKER
"Dear King, Your people have to eat;
So, I'll serve up their bread and meat.
I'll be as happy as can be
As waitress, cook, or maitre d'."

WRITER
"Since writing was your gift to me,
I'll use it to help others see
I'll tell with plain or rhyming words
The greatest Story ever heard."

MINISTER
A humble lad then bowed his head
And speaking very softly, said,
"A minister—that's what I'll do
To gently lead lost souls to you."

The King was grinning ear to ear,
For that's just what He'd hoped to hear.
Each child would be a servant true
By serving Him and others, too.

"This world will be a happy place,"
The King said with a smiling face.
"All honest work is good and right,
But serving others brings delight."